Down & Dirty
The Secrets of Soil

Why Do Most Plants Need Soil?

by Ellen Lawrence

Consultant:

Shawn W. Wallace
Department of Earth and Planetary Sciences
American Museum of Natural History
New York, New York

BEARPORT PUBLISHING

New York, New York

Credits

Cover, © Romolo Tavani/Shutterstock; 4, © Bonnie Fink/Shutterstock; 5, © Jorg Hackemann/Shutterstock, © Tom Reichner/Shutterstock, © MVPhoto/Shutterstock, and © D. Kucharski K. Kucharska/Shutterstock; 6T, © Shi Yali/Shutterstock; 6B, © Dino Martino Photography/Shutterstock; 7, © Andreas Altenburger/Shutterstock; 8, © Filipe B. Varela/Shutterstock; 9, © maxhomand/iStock and © Orla/Shutterstock; 10, © Aggie II/Shutterstock; 11, © tormentor3/Shutterstock; 12, © Casther/Shutterstock; 13, © Hugh Lansdown/Shutterstock and © Dr. Jeremy Burgess/Science Photo Library; 14L, © Hhelene/Shutterstock; 14R, © Richard Griffin/Shutterstock; 15, © Peter Etchells/Shutterstock; 16T, © Tanor/Shutterstock; 16B, © Drew Fitzgibbon/Shutterstock; 17, © Cody H.; 17TR, © hwongcc/Shutterstock; 18, © Wayne Hutchinson/FLPA; 19, © John Eveson/FLPA; 20T, © Jose Ignacio Soto/Shutterstock; 20B, © Vlad Teodor/Shutterstock; 21, © Viorel Sima/Shutterstock; 22, © Ruby Tuesday Books, © Ekaterina Garyuk/Shutterstock, and © Africa Studio/Shutterstock; 23TL, © Krit Leoniz/Shutterstock; 23TC, © Gunnar Pippel/Shutterstock; 23TR, © Thalang Itsaranggura/Shutterstock; 23BL, © Blue Sky Studio/Shutterstock; 23BC, © FotograFFF/Shutterstock; 23BR, © varuna/Shutterstock.

Publisher: Kenn Goin
Senior Editor: Joyce Tavolacci
Creative Director: Spencer Brinker
Design: Emma Randall
Photo Researcher: Ruby Tuesday Books Ltd

Library of Congress Cataloging-in-Publication Data

Lawrence, Ellen, 1967– author.
  Why do most plants need soil? / By Ellen Lawrence.
     pages cm. — (Down & dirty : the secrets of soil)
  Summary: "In this book readers will learn why plants need soil."— Provided by publisher.
  Audience: Ages 4–8
  Includes bibliographical references and index.
  ISBN 978-1-62724-837-2 (library binding) — ISBN 1-62724-837-4 (library binding)
  1. Plant-soil relationships—Juvenile literature. 2. Plants—Juvenile literature. 3. Soil biology—Juvenile literature. I. Title.
  S591.3.L39 2016
  580—dc23
                                    2015015257

For more information, write to Bearport Publishing Company, Inc., 45 West 21st Street, Suite 3B, New York, New York 10010. Printed in the United States of America.

10 9 8 7 6 5 4 3 2

Contents

Parts of a Forest

Tall, leafy trees grow in a forest.

Birds, squirrels, and insects make their homes in the trees.

Beneath the trees are ferns, wildflowers, and other small plants.

There's one important part of the forest, however, that doesn't often get noticed—the soil.

Without soil, the forest would not exist. Let's find out why.

ferns

What do you think soil is made of?

squirrel

woodpecker

Millions of tiny creatures such as worms, beetles, and ants live on the ground and in the soil of a forest.

worm

What Is Soil?

Most plants, including trees, need soil in order to live and grow.

So what is soil made of?

The main **ingredient** is tiny pieces of rock.

Soil is also made from bits of dead plants.

When plants die or leaves fall from trees, they rot and become part of the soil.

pieces of rock in soil

rotting leaves

When a bird or other animal dies, its body rots. Then tiny pieces of feathers or fur, bones, and other body parts become part of the soil.

a dead owl in a forest

Support from the Ground Up

Why is soil so important for most plants?

Plants have **roots** that grow into the soil.

A plant's roots spread out to firmly hold it in the ground.

The roots help prevent the plant from blowing over when it's windy.

They also keep the plant from toppling over if its branches or flowers get too heavy.

roots

Plant roots have another important job to do. What do you think this is?

The roots of some trees spread out over a huge area. The roots may be two or three times the length of the tree's branches.

roots

Soil, Water, and Roots

Soil helps plants in another important way.

Plants need water to survive.

When it rains, water trickles down and collects in tiny spaces in the soil.

A plant's roots reach down into these spaces.

The roots then soak up all the water the plant needs.

young oak tree

A plant needs water in order to make food so it can grow. Inside its leaves, a plant turns water, a **gas** from the air called carbon dioxide, and sunlight into a sugary food.

Getting Nutrients

Plants also need **nutrients** to grow and be healthy.

Where do they get nutrients? Soil!

Rotting plant **material** and dead animals add lots of nutrients to soil.

Plants take in these nutrients with their roots.

How do you think soil helps new plants grow?

carrot plant

roots

A large tree may have roots as thick as a person's leg. Growing out of the thick roots are thin, hair-like roots. These tiny roots take in water and nutrients from soil.

thick roots

These tiny roots grow underground. They are thinner than human hairs!

Starting Out as Seeds

Many plants start out as seeds.

After a seed is planted in soil, it grows tiny roots.

Then a little green shoot pushes up out of the ground.

The little plant takes in water and nutrients from the soil.

The plant gets bigger and bigger until it's fully grown!

bean shoot

seed

roots

bean seeds

fully grown bean plants

Seeds come in many shapes, sizes, and colors.

No Soil?

Some plants don't need any soil to grow.

A group of plants called epiphytes (EP-*uh*-fites) often grow on trees instead of in soil.

The roots of these plants attach to tree trunks or branches.

Some epiphytes have leaves that form a cup.

Rainwater collects inside the cup and is soaked up by the plant.

an epiphyte growing on a tree trunk

water collected in an epiphyte's cup

Tillandsias, or air plants, are epiphytes that take in water through their leaves. These plants can grow almost anywhere—even on power lines!

tillandsias

tillandsia plants

Poor Soil, Healthy Soil

In some places around the world, the soil is dry and has few nutrients.

Farmers who live in these places have a hard time growing crops.

However, there are ways to make the soil healthier for plants.

Compost is made up of dead plant matter and is filled with nutrients.

When farmers add compost to soil, they make the soil healthier for their crops.

a farmer in Africa adds compost to soil

compost

Animal dung contains lots of nutrients that plants need. Sometimes farmers spread dung on their fields to make the soil healthy.

animal dung

Why do you think it's important that farmers have healthy soil for growing crops?

Food and Soil

When soil is healthy, farmers can grow many crops.

These crops include wheat and oats for making bread and cereal.

Farmers also grow tasty vegetables and fruit.

We might not think of soil when we bite into a slice of toast or a tomato.

Without soil, however, we wouldn't have most of the foods we eat every day!

a tractor cutting wheat

a farmer growing tomatoes

Without plants, we wouldn't have milk and other dairy foods, such as cheese and yogurt. That's because in order to make milk, cows and goats must eat grass and other plants.

a dairy cow eating grass

Science Lab

Be a Soil Scientist

In this experiment, you will investigate how well plants grow in four different types of soil.

> ### You will need:
> - Four types of soil
> - Four flowerpots
> - Eight bean seeds
> - A small shovel
> - A marker
> - A notebook and pencil

Soil 1

potting soil from a garden center

Soil 2

soil from a garden or yard where plants are growing

Soil 3

soil from an area where plants aren't growing

Soil 4

sandy soil

Soil Experiment Step-by-Step

Ask a grown-up to help you buy potting soil, flowerpots, and bean seeds online or from a garden center.

1. Collect four types of soil.

2. Using a small shovel, fill each flowerpot with a different type of soil. Use a marker to label each pot.

3. Place two bean seeds in each pot, cover them with soil, and press down gently.

Soil 1

4. Place the pots in a sunny window. Water the seeds to keep the soil moist. Then wait and see what happens!

- **Which soil do you think the plants will grow best in? Why? Write down your prediction in a notebook.**
- **When the bean plants start to grow, which one grows fastest? Which looks healthiest?**
- **Why do you think your prediction did or did not match what happened?**

Science Words

compost (KOM-pohst) natural material that has rotted and can be added to soil to improve its quality

gas (GASS) matter that floats in air and is neither a liquid nor a solid; most gases, such as carbon dioxide, are invisible

ingredient (in-GREE-dee-uhnt) one of the materials that something is made from

material (muh-TIHR-ee-uhl) any substance from which things are made

nutrients (NOO-tree-uhnts) vitamins, minerals, and other substances needed by living things to grow and be healthy

roots (ROOTS) underground plant parts that take in water and nutrients from the soil; roots often spread out in the soil to hold a plant in place

23

Index

Read More

Flanagan, Alice K. *Soil (Simply Science)*. Minneapolis, MN: Compass Point Books (2001).

MacAulay, Kelley. *Why Do We Need Soil? (Natural Resources Close-Up)*. New York: Crabtree (2014).

Waldron, Melanie. *Roots (Plant Parts)*. North Mankato, MN: Heinemann-Raintree (2014).

Learn More Online

To learn more about plants and soil, visit
www.bearportpublishing.com/Down&Dirty

About the Author

Ellen Lawrence lives in the United Kingdom. Her favorite books to write are those about animals and nature. In fact, the first book Ellen bought for herself, when she was six years old, was the story of a gorilla named Patty Cake that was born in New York's Central Park Zoo.

24